BUDAPEST

and its environs

19.09.2012

Dear Nicole and Emily!

Welcome to Hungary and to Horzhy. We wish you a wonderful and enjoyable visit and hope you will come back many more times!

Lots of love,

Dad-Opi and Irene

With text by
Balázs Dercsényi

BUDAPEST
and its environs

MERHAVIA, BUDAPEST

Published by MERHAVIA LTD.
(1139 Budapest, Teve u. 41.).
The director of the press is responsible for the publication.

PHOTOGRAPHY CREDITS:

Róbert Hack	14, 90, 91, 92, 131, 183, 201
András Hász	16, 17, 64, 81, 89, 176, 177, 179, 206
Tibor Hortobágyi	18, 21, 22, 24, 26, 28, 33, 36, 50, 54, 61, 63, 66, 67, 68, 82, 100, 103, 116, 117, 118, 120, 126, 130, 152, 154, 157, 158, 159, 160, 162, 180, 181, 184
Ottó Kaiser	38, 39, 42, 43, 44, 51
Tamás Mihalik	65

With the co-operation of the ARCHIVES OF MAGYAR KÉPEK LTD., BUDAPEST:

Lajos Köteles	85, 87, 115
Attila Mudrák	93, 94, 95, 96, 97, 98
Károly Szelényi	11, 15, 29, 31, 46, 53, 55, 56, 57, 76, 99, 101, 104, 106, 107, 109, 110, 111, 119, 121, 123, 128, 132, 135, 137, 138, 139, 142, 143, 144, 146, 148, 149, 150, 151, 153, 161, 163, 167, 168, 169, 175, 187, 192, 194, 197, 198, 199, 200, 203, 207
Levente Szepsy Szűcs	5, 45

With the co-operation of AVALON GRAPHICS Picture Agency, BUDAPEST:

Ágoston Bányai	79, 83, 84, 86, 202
Ferenc Mayer	6, 7, 13, 25, 34, 41, 70, 102, 196
Péter Molnár	1
Ferenc Papp	108
Dr. József Szabó	133
Dénes Szőcs	3, 4, 8, 10, 12, 19, 23, 27, 30, 32, 35, 40, 48, 49, 58, 59, 60, 62, 69, 71, 72, 73, 80, 105, 112, 113, 114, 124, 125, 127, 134, 140, 141, 145, 147, 155, 156, 171, 172, 173, 182, 185, 186, 188, 189, 190, 191, 193, 195, 205, dust jacket and hard cover photograph
Béla Tóth	2, 9, 37, 52, 75, 77, 78, 88, 122, 170, 174, 178
Avalon archives	20, 47, 74, 129, 136, 164, 165, 166, 204, 208

On the dust jacket:
View of the Parliament from the Royal Palace, Buda (front)
Statue of Queen Elisabeth (Sisi) with the statue of St. Gellért in the backgrond (back)

On the hard cover:
Mosaic picture of the Country Arms at Clark Ádám square

Colour separation: *GMN Stúdió, Budapest*
Printing: *Pauker Printing House Ltd., Budapest, 2004*
Supervised by: *Gábor Vértes, director*

ISBN 963 9172 31 6

The following more than two hundred photos reflect truly Budapest at the beginning of the 21st century, however, its historical layers shall also be mentioned, which sometimes hidden, sometimes apparently determine the today's view of the capital established in 1872 by uniting Óbuda, Pest and Buda. The oldest or the bottom layer is of the Roman age. Some years before the birth of Christ Emperor Augustus occupied the area located to the south and north of the Danube, that crosses the Carpathian basin. On the right and the left riversides the Romans built up the 'limes' consisting of watch-towers, fortresses and military camp to defend their empire from the Barbarians' attacks. Later, from the 9th century, our sovereigns settled their people in Aquincum under the protection of the high walls of the military amphitheatre of the town. The first sprouts of Pest appeared at the walls of Contra-Aquincum having protected the most important crossing place, the ferry of Tabán. The importance of Óbuda was based on the fact, that among the remains from the Roman age and by using them settlements were established by merchants and tradesmen, then royal courts, monasteries and churches were constructed, as well. The first medieval layer of the town, the first golden era of Óbuda and Pest was ceased by the Tartar invasion in 1241 resulting in terrible destruction and massacre.

The reconstruction and the settlement on the well-defendable Castle Hill gave opening to the flourishing medieval age. Quarters were established by Germans and Hungarians on the hill, civic houses, parish-churches and monasteries were built under the protection of the town walls and years 100 later the town became suitable to be the seat of King Louis I of the Anjou dynasty of Naples. He and the sovereigns following him developed the town on the Castle Hill to become the centre of the Carpathian basin, their palace erected on the southern part became more and more imposing. In the civic town aristocrats built up brilliant residences and the churches and dwelling-houses were decorated with European rank works of art in the Gothic and early-Renaissance styles. The Empire being governed from here deeply protruded into the Balkan Peninsula, reached the Adriatic Sea and Louis I became the King of Poland, too.

At dawn of the modern times, from 1541, the tripartite city was in the possession of the Turks over one and half hundred years, and their presence brought double 'fruits': the brilliant palaces and civic houses were slowly deteriorating while the churches, monasteries were transformed into mosques. In 1686 the unified Christian armies liberated Buda and later on the whole country, however, the medieval brilliance of the Hungarian kingdom has never come back, the nation's freedom and independence was regained only after a long period, as the Habsburgs reigned over the Carpathian basin. Óbuda became a manorial centre and Buda was transformed into a quiet small town, though over the medieval ruins a Baroque palace was built – in a modest manner – for the palatine. The revival of Pest was more dynamic and the area surrounded by town walls became rather tight. Everything, created after forcing out the Turks was complying with the Baroque style, although the country could not keep up with the brilliance of Prague or Vienna for a long time.

Then the 19th century set in and Pest started developing rapidly: the conscious urban development resulted in the organized order of newly built Neoclassical public buildings, churches, civic houses and hotels, which were stretching well beyond the town walls. Due to the unexampled efforts exerted by István Széchenyi, 'the greatest Hungarian', the Chain Bridge was born, representing the first permanent connection between Buda and Pest, i.e. Trans-Danubia and other counties. By the middle of the century Pest had become unambiguously the centre of the country.

In 1849 the union of the Austrian Emperor and the Russian Tsar suppressed the fight for the national independence, whose leaders were condemned to peregrinate or to death, and the Hungarian progress was retarded for two decades. However, during the years of sorrow, fear and terror, the thought of the Austro-Hungarian Monarchy was born and the Compromise came into existence with the demand for a co-capital. In 1872 Óbuda, Buda and Pest were united, and by the last decades of the 19th century Budapest became an adequate capital in the Carpathian basin. The city was not only the centre of public administration in the country being essentially larger that time than now, but became the focus of industry, commerce, communication, art, education and, last but not least, of architecture. The new Budapest born in the spirit of Historicity and Secessionisme, which lived their flourishing life until the First World War. It is true, however, that several historical layers and values from different periods live in harmony .

2

3

From Hungary firstly the *Castle Hill* of Buda and the *lines of houses on the two Danube banks* were registered in the *UNESCO World Heritage Sites* to recognize the importance of the values the centre of the medieval Hungarian kingdom has conveyed from the 13th century *(2)*.

Two parish-churches are rising from the civic town conserving medieval structures. Their construction commenced in the middle of the 13th century. The civic town consists of streets with smaller houses of medieval dimensions carrying many times Gothic or Renaissance details. Some larger buildings are inserted among them, for example a monastery, the large block of the Archives or a caserne. The *Castle Hill* ends with the *Royal Palace*. It is a cultural centre including museums and the first public library of the country. In the picture the row of houses on the left river bank and the bridges are appearing, the first is the *Chain Bridge* inaugurated in 1849, the further one is the graceful *Elisabeth Bridge* from the 1960s.

The function of the Chain Bridge was completed by the construction of the *Tunnel* in 1856. The engineer's structure behind the Neoclassical portal under the Castle Hill was realized according to the plans of Adam Clark, constructor of the Chain Bridge *(3)*.

4

5

6

The area between the civic quarter and the Royal Palace was beeing built in mainly from the 18th century. At first the *Carmelite* order erected a *cloister* and a *church*, but the latter was transformed into *theatre* in 1787. Farther off, the *Neoclassical Sándor palace* was built at the beginning of the 19th century. It was the Prime Minister's headquarters from 1867 to 1945 and today is the seat of the President of the Republic *(4)*.

The museum buildings are separated from the civic quarter by an *ornamented fence in the neo-Baroque style (6)*. On the promenade before the museums, from where a splendid panorama opens, stays the *equestrian statue of Prince Eugene of Savoy (5)*, commander-in-chief of the Christian armies forcing out the Turks.

In *Szentháromság (Holy Trinity) Square (7,9)*, in the centre of the civic town of Buda the eponymous *statue composition* in the middle was erected between 1712–14.

After the retreat of the Tartars in 1242 the area was in terrible conditions. It was proven, however, that fortresses were almost unconquerable by the Tartar armies. For this reason and the reconstruction, the settlements required the protection of walls. After his return Béla (Adalbert) IV, escaped from the lost battle of Muhi to Dalmatia granted privileges for the citizens of Pest. In 1243, on hearing the intention of the Tartars to attack anew, the settlement on the Castle Hill started from two directions: Germans arrived from Pest to the area of Szentháromság Square, while the Hungarians settled on the northern plateau, and the reinforcement of Castle Hill started, as well. Under the protection of the cliff and the town walls the Germans started constructing their parish-church in the mid-1250s, and nearby the Buda house of the Dominicans was completed in 1254. At that time the Hungarian parish-church had already been under construction and the Franciscans feeling themselves at home first of all among the poor, erected their monastery, too. The *remains of the Dominicans' building* are built into the two wings of the *Hotel Hilton* and its place is indicated by the church tower rising out of the building, north of the *Matthias Church (9,10)*.

The houses in the streets, running on to the square formed a closed space with the Matthias Church, whose towers rose from among there. Since its reconstruction at the end of the 1800s, the church has been standing independently.

The construction of the splendid *early-Baroque Town Hall (7)* was finished around 1710 and required five medieval houses to be destroyed, but this number reached a dozen in 1904 because of the grandiose neo-Gothic *House of the Hungarian Culture (10)*.

Not all that existed before the Turkish era (1541) has disappeared. In *Tárnok Street two buildings (8)* and further details, e.g. *sedilia from the 14th–15th century* can be traced.

9

Behind the sanctuary of the Matthias Church from the Fishermen's Bastion we can get a find view over the Danube and Pest. If poem exists in the architecture, it is like that. Frigyes Schulek, dreamer of the cathedral of Buda, thought to connect the Danube bank and the hill with elegant stairs by closing them with a system of bastions at the sanctuary of the cathedral. From this plan the *Fishermen's Bastion* and the upper part of the steps were realized. Schulek, being well experienced in the history of architecture with lively fantasy, imagined the fortress wall section with bastions protected by fishermen and articulated by towers, arcades, arched steps, tabernacles with statues, etc. *(11)*. It is certain that the original bastion was more severe and defendable, but less civilised. Schlulek's dream, however, enriches the programme of tourists visiting the Castle District: the wiev is grandiose from the terraces on Víziváros (Water Town) and the Danube with the island and bridge named after St. Margaret, as well as the Parliament and innumerable houses extending towards the far hills.

11

12

14

15

In the bay of the bastion stands the *equestrian statue of St. Stephen (12)*, the founder of state and our first king (István, 1000–1038) canonized at the end of the 11th century. The statue was shaped by Alajos Stróbl, one of the most popular artists of his age, in 1906.

Szentháromság Square the most representative building is the *Matthias Church (17)*. The square bore medieval marks until the end of the 19th century, then it was opened towards the Danube. The church was consecrated to Our Lady in the second trimester of the 13th century as a three ailed basilica with included transept, polygon shaped sanctuary and ribbed cross vaults borne by column and pillar heads.

The remained stone carvings outline the North French Gothic style. The West European influence on Buda was mediated by South Germany and Austria. In 1309 Charles Robert of Anjou, the winner of the struggle for the throne following the dying out of the Árpád dinasty, was crowned here. The 'Dormition of the Virgin' gate reflecting South German influence was constructed by his son, king Louis I around 1370. At that time new sanctuaries were built and the former basilica was transformed into 'hall-church' by raising the aisles. Only the large windows placed into the lateral walls illuminated the nave. This way an extended and more attractive space was created *(14)*. Not only the German citizens participated in the construction of the church: both the sovereigns and the aristocrats appearing in a greater and greater number in the town erected chapels around the nave.

The church received its popular name after Matthias – the son of János Hunyadi, the winner of the battle of Nándorfehérvár – who paid the first visit in the church after his election to king on the ice of the Danube and his both marriages were celebrated here. He also constructed an oratory for his numerous royal households. The number '1470' on the higher tower indicates the date of the reconstruction of the church during the Matthias era.

In 1541 the Turks occupied Buda by ruse. The installations and the figural ornaments of the church were removed, where those were accessible, and the building was transformed into a mosque. After the retaking of Buda in 1686 the building was in good condition, only its installation missed. At first it was granted to the Franciscans then to the Jesuits. They squeezed the church among new buildings (a monastery and a seminary) and provided it with installations.

In 1773, the year of the suppressing the orders, the town got back the church under its supremacy, but the building preserved its historical role: when archaeologists opened the deteriorated royal basilica in Székesfehérvár they found the remains of *King Béla III and his French wife Anna Chatillon*, the Matthias Church was considered suitable and worthy as *final resting-place for the royal couple (15)*. In the year of the Compromise (1867) Francis Joseph and

16

Elisabeth were also crowned Hungary's King and Queen here.

Between 1874 and 1896 Frigyes Schulek reconstructed the church for the Millennium: released it from the squeeze of the surrounding buildings, restored the 13th-century sanctuaries and replaced the 18th-century Baroque style installations with medieval-like ones. Schulek made the building more attractive: the interior surface received old-like *ornamental decoration (16)* and the exterior surface was covered with neo-Gothic details, designed by himself. The *Matthias Church* follows in most of its details the medieval churches, but the solutions of the 13th century are prevailing and, as a result, a wonderful temple dominates the silhouette of the hill *(17,18)*.

17

18

20

To the left from the cathedral, the elegant façade of the *Hotel Hilton* was constructed in 1784 *(18)*. The tower of the Dominican monastery- church with the *relief of King Matthias* from the year of 1485 *(19)* rises up from the hotel building.

Some details of the monastery and the church may be discovered inside the hotel: the church space and the Dominican cloister give a good idea about the monastery of Buda. From the church space – place for musical performances in summer – a *particular view* opens on the neo-Gothic building of the Parliament *(20)*. There are sother sights in the sanctuary, too, e.g. a bronze statue shaping two Dominican friars, Julian and Gerard who received an order in 1235 to search

19

for Hungarians in the country of origin, in the Ural. Gerard died during the journey, but the mission of Julian ended successfully. The composition illustrates Julian supporting the dying Gerard; they both are looking to the East, towards the country of origin.

The today's appearance of the Castle District is determined by the constructions from the 18th and 19th centuries. However, in the course of the restorations made after the World War II almost all dwelling-houses revealed some details from their past. Smaller and greater medieval fragments make it evident, that some buildings survived the Turkish era and the sieges. These were preserved and covered later on with *Baroque walls*, *plastered ornaments* and *frescoes*, with adorned door and windows frames, and artistic *wrought iron works* on them *(21)*.

The narrow streets of the Castle District run into small squares in which statues are standing and reminding. The square before the Hotel Hilton named after András Hess – the first printer of Buda – is decorated with the statue of *Pope Innocent XI (Benedetto Odescalchi) (22)*. His role was determining in the organization and financing of the Saint League against the Turks and in the liberation of Vienna in 1683 and Buda in 1686.

From here two streets lead to Bécsi kapu (Vienna Gate) Square. The right one was in the possession of the Jewry. Among some Baroque palaces their synagogue can be found there hidden in a simple house from the 15th century, which is a rarity in Central Europe.

One of the palaces, with a wonderful Baroque façade, adorned arms and ornamented balcony, used to belong to the Erdődy family, who – similarly to many others – thought, they also deserved a palace, worthy of their status, in the neighbourhood of the palatine.

In the curved street small civic houses and a prison in the Baroque style are still standing, and at the end of the street the town gate is warding the old road leading to Vienna.

21

22

23

The *church* in Kapisztrán Square was erected in honour of *Maria Magdalen* by the Hungarian founders of the town and was deteriorated during the World War II in the course of the siege of Buda. Only its tower, some base walls and one of its reconstructed windows remained *(23)*. The elegant Gothic church was constructed in the 1260s and used by the catholic and protestant believers during the Turkish rule until the beginning of the 17th century, when the conquerors transformed its interior to a triumphal mosque. After 1686 the damaged church was granted to the Franciscans who demolished its sanctuary and nave, then reconstructed it in the Baroque style.

The Franciscans could not enjoy the fruits of their work for long. Towards the end of the 18th century the 'hatted king', Austrian Emperor Joseph II, follower of the absolutism suppressed the monastic orders, and the Franciscan church was granted to the garrison.

Some streets are closing with the sight of the Matthias Church, such as *Fortuna Street (24)*, named after the rest house 'Goddess Fortuna'. Nowadays a museum presents here the history of the entertainment and catering in Hungary. It is worth to have a look into some *courtyards*, too...*(25)*. The small *Bécsi kapu Square* with its houses from end of the 18th and the beginning of the 19th century is situated at the foot of the large neo-Romanesque building of the Hungarian National Archives. In the Middle Ages the most important weekday market, namely the Saturday market, was held here. The square is decorated by the *statue of Ferenc Kazinczy (26)*, set up in 1936, commemorating to the poet and leader personality of the language reform in the 19th century.

24

25

Bécsi kapu Square is a one-minute walk from *Kapisztrán Square*, which is renowned not only for its medieval Hungarian parish-church but also the Neoclassical building dominating the area, the *War History Museum*. The building of a simple and strict appearance was erected in 1847 and transformed from barracks into museum in 1929. Its exhibitions present the history of the Hungarian Royal

27

28

29

Army during the 19th and 20th centuries. The *entrance to the museum (30)* opens in the Western promenade of the Castle District.

The *promenade (29)* is an important part of the fortress, where the most beautiful view opens from on Krisztina town, the Gellért Hill, the mountains of Buda and the 529-meters-high János Hill with a fortress-like tower on its top. In the Middle Ages the hillsides of Buda were hunting-grounds, their spring-waters, once used by the inhabitants, are marked today by curiously shaped small houses.

At the beginning of the 19th century the wealthy citizens of Pest and Buda possessed a domicile in the town and a villa on the hills. From the years of 1850 more and more people inhabited the hills and this process is still going on. In the places of forests, orchards and vineyards villas and blocks of freehold flats have been constructed.

In addition to the belle-view there are other sights among the shading trees of the promenade, e.g. the *turbaned column* made *by the Zsolnay Porcelain Factory* of Pécs and donated in 1972 for the centenary of the capital *(31).*

At Kapisztrán Square, at which it is worthy to have a look at the City Hall, on the façade of a small house a refinely placed *woman figure* illustrates that at this place *formerly nuns lived (28).*

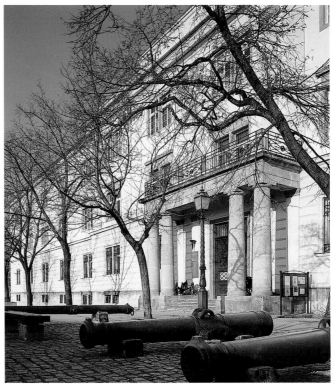

30

31

32

33

Most *houses in the civic quarter* were constructed in the Rococo, the High Baroque and Neoclassical styles or represent the works of the period passed from the second half of the 19th century. Among one-storeyed houses some public buildings of more levels can also be found. The restorations after the World War II made it possible for archaeologists and art historians not only to examine the past by documents, old drawings and photos taken on buildings, but also to explore their walls and plasters. It has been evidenced, that several *buildings in the Gothic style* originate from the Middle Ages with details from the 14th–15th centuries. This can be seen *in Országház Street* on the houses dating back to the 15th century, with *mullioned windows*, *arched dividing cornices* or *consoles* bearing the closed balcony *(32, 33)*. The appearance of the street does not reflect always the inner space, e.g. at the beginning of Ország-ház Street, where *Gothic sedilia and arches* can be found *in the doorways (35)*. As to our present knowledge, such monuments exist only in Buda and Sopron. However, there are *two-storeyed civic houses (36)* from the 15th century, e.g. the former *Town Hall (34)* with its harmonic and elegant pre-Baroque façade, which was constructed in the place of five medieval civic houses.

Count András Hadik lieutenant general, who descended on Berlin and held the town to ransom in 1757, *'is riding'* opposite to the house. The *Ruszwurm patisserie*, shown on the left side in the picture functions in a civic house from 1827 and is very popular either for its products or its *installations in the Empire style (34)*.

34

35

36

37

38

39

The construction of the István tower, beeing the first royal edifice, may be esteemed around the mid-15ᵗʰ century. The builder was the brother of King Louis I of Anjou. King Sigismund's palaces were erected northerly and their brilliance was worthy of the sovereign gaining the title of Holy Roman Emperor, as well.

King Matthias (1458–92) spent his money abundantly for his palace especially when he married his second wife, Beatrix of Naples. Due to the majestic lady accustomed to the Renaissance culture, the art of the Italian quattrocento gained ground in Hungary. *Matthias' palace* was embellished with red marble panelled ceilings, windows and door frames, decorated stoves, ceramic floor tiles made according to the craftsmen of Faenza and in the courtyard and on the fortress sides with *ornamented gardens (41)*.

The *large circular bastion (Rondella) and the Mace tower (37, 39)* were constructed at the very end of the 15ᵗʰ century utilizing the modern technique of warfare. However, to the South of the borders of the kingdom the Turks were already dominating, and finally they had taken Buda for 145 years. Neverthelss, they were interested only in the fortress, all the rest started slowly deteriorating, and most of the valuables were carried to Constantinople.

When Buda was relieved from the Turkish rule significant remains of the Renaissance palace were still standing. By filling in these, a modest building was built up for the soldiery between 1715–38, followed by a more serious palace for the palatine acting for the Austrian sovereigns.

Having concluded the Compromise in 1867 it was necessary for the capital anew to have an imposing Royal Palace and in 1881 the most reputed architect, Miklós Ybl was charged with the reconstruction of the edifice. He doubled the 18ᵗʰ-century building northwards and, as a large 'emphasis', put a dome in the middle axis of the horizontal mass. At the end of the World War II the palace was seriously damaged and its installations were destroyed. Before its restoration investigations were made after the traces of the medieval royal architecture. The parts being suitable for authentic reconstruction, i.e. the *Rondella, the gate tower (37)*, the hall of knights, a *closed balcony (38), the medieval protecting works (37)* were restored and *one of the Renaissance gardens was reinstalled (41)*. The Palace quarter received *cultural task: museums (40) and the national library*, founded in 1802, were re-opened here.

40

41

42

43

In the *Budapest History Museum* the restored *Royal Chapel (42)* of the Anjou age from around 1360, details of the *façade of the medieval palace (43)*, as well as ornamental and figural *carvings*, e.g. a *noble man from the early-15th century (44)* are displayed together with many other relics: among others red marble building decorations of the Matthias era, ceramic floor bricks and the restored early-Renaissance stove can be seen.

Another sight of the Budapest History Museum functioning in the southern wing is the *'statue cemetery'* re-

44

vealed in 1974. The defaced statues once were used for filling in sites and buried, perhaps to rise once, to illustrate in some way the art of the 15th century. The statues figuring people of different kind, status and sex were prepared probably with decorative purposes for an impressive gallery in the newly constructed palace of the sovereign. Their masters worked under different artistic influences, one was inspired rather by Prague and the other might have been an excellent follower of the Austrian plastic art at the beginning of the 15th century.

The Baroque palace, erected on the plateau formed over the medieval

45

46

47

palace or rather out of its ruins, may be perceived with difficulties because of its transformation, enlargement or deterioration.

Today, having been restored from the senseless destruction of the World War II, it is *a complex of museums*. Beside the museum presenting the past of the capital, the long wing opening onto the Da-nube is the home of the national painting and sculptural art. The *Hungarian National Gallery* was founded in 1957 primarily for the presentation of the Hungarian *fine arts of the 19th and 20th centuries (45, 46)*, but the exhibition of the secular and ecclesiastical arts of the 18th-century Baroque is also valuable, offering a look into the age of the *Gothic winged-altars (47)*, stone- and wood-carvings, too.

Due to the exploring works occasional exhibitions and foreign collections may also be visited. The *Ludwig Museum of Budapest* in the northern wing of the palace complex overlooking the civic quarter is the home of the contemporary art, while the Széchényi National Library building on the western side giving upon Krisztina town stands approximately at the place where once a wonderful Renaissance garden served King Matthias and his households at the end of the 15th century.

48

On leaving the Castle District, the civic town and the former Royal Palace, towards Tabán, we can have a look back on the *large circular bastion and the Mace tower (51)* or the *hillside reinforced with fortress walls (49)*. At the foot of the Elisabeth Bridge – where Gellért Hill and Castle Hill tighten the river and the Ördög-árok (The Devil's Ditch) collecting the sources of the Buda hills flows into the Danube – was the most suitable crossing place. For the protection of the ferry a Roman fortress was constructed, since the barbarians frequented the place, too.

The conquering Hungarians occupied this area at first in order to ensure their crossing. In the first half of the 13th century mainly the Pest riverside developed, but at the foot of Castle Hill in the long valley villages were established, the ruins of their chapels have only been preserved.

During the Turkish occupation other nations accompanying the Sultan, mainly the Slavs settled in here. Small houses framed the meandering streets: this was the Tabán – the last remain of which was the church of the orthodox Serb inhabitants – destroyed under the World War II. Along the road leading into the valley, the *Arany Szarvas (Golden Deer) Café (50)*, today restaurant can be found, which was constructed at the beginning of the 19th century.

In its neighbourhood the Museum of Medical History receives its guests in the house of birth of the

phisicien Ignác Semmelweis, 'the saver of mothers', and gives some idea about the medical past of the Carpathian basin.

Two valuable constructions drawing the attention of the visitor here. One of them is the *retaining wall and the artistic garden edifice* connected to the Castle Hill *(48)*, the other towered building is the *former pump house* with water machines to elevate the water out of the Danube up to the Royal Palace. Miklós Ybl, a leading architect at the end of the 19th century, constructed both buildings, so his bust has been placed here.

The monument complex of Buda Castle, together with the row of houses along the Danube banks appeare in the UNESCO World Heritage Sites Register. From 2002 the ensemble has been extended with Andrássy Avenue and other valuable Hungarian buildings and places, e.g. the Benedictine Abbey of Pannonhalma, early-Christian tomb edifices in Pécs, the dripstone caves of Aggtelek, the natural and architectural values of Hortobágy, the old village of Hollókő, the mountains producing the reputed vine of Tokaj, the Fertő lake and its narrower environment with natural specialities and registered monumental relics.

50

51

53

The aerial photo presents the area of Budapest registered in the World Heritage Sites, the southern section of the Danube banks and the *Gellért Hill (52)*. To the left in the picture, in Tabán a medieval Turkish bath, the *Rác Medical Bath (53)* can be found.

The hill has taken its name after the missionary bishop arriving from Venice. In 1046 the pagan Hungarians fighting against the adoption of the Christianity captured the *Benedictine Gellért* and precipitated its body from the steep cliffs. His corps is guarded in the twin-towered parish-church on the opposite river bank and *to his memory a statue* was erected *surrounded by a colonnade* on the hillside *(54)*.

The walls of the *Citadella on the hilltop* were built in the mid-1800s to form the part of a fortress system in order to control the town revolting against the Habsburgs in 1848–49. Its role was ceased soon, in 1875, and since then, the fortress has stayed incopletely. Later a statue composition illustrating the liberty was placed at its end from the Danube.

The mountain is rising out from its environment by 130 meters, but looks to be higher. In its bowels

52

dozens of thermal sources provide water for the baths located at the hillfoot. Not only the Turks, but the new citizens of the liberated Buda enjoyed them, as well, and so it is nowadays, when they serve three baths, from which one was mentioned above.

The second *bath* is the *Rudas* at the foot of the Elisabeth Bridge. The space covered with cupola forms its central core. It was constructed in 1566 and named Green Column Bath by Musztafa Szokollu Pasha. The thermal water of a temperature of 27–48° C is used for curing rheumatic, arterial, neurological diseases.

A further speciality there is the chapel hollowed out the hill: it is in the Paulines' use, whose order is named after St. Paul, the Hermit.

One of our most famed *thermal bath complex* is named after Bishop *Gellért (56)*, and so as to enjoy the swimming-pool with artificial waves and the sparkling bath more completely, a hotel was constructed for the more affluent guests.

The hotel and its bath were completed in 1918 and their style and luxury remind us to the Baroque era. As for the bath, the architects referred even to a more ancient time by borrowing from the classic forms, i.e. the thermae of Rome. The system of the Roman imperial period is linked with the immoderate and decorative works of the *applied arts in the Secession style* from the beginning of the 1900s *(55)*.

The *environment of the hotel (57)* shall also be mentioned: the most important educational centre of engineers constructed on the turning of the 19th–20th centuries and *one of the most beautiful bridges* can be found here. This latter – inaugurated by *its eponym Emperor Francis Joseph* in 1896 – reflects both the engineering knowledge and the aesthetic requirements of its architect.

On the opposite side of the bridge the biggest market hall of the capital receives its buyers.

55

56

58

59

In Buda the *Castle Museum of Nagytétény* should be mentioned from the large scale of sights to the south of the Castle District. Roman traces can also be found here: the stones of the fortress named Campona drawn on the settlers and their masters in the Middle Ages. In the 15th century the Tétényi family made use of the roman remains as stone quarry and from the stones constructed a manor house. In the following century the major part of the house was deteriorated, but around 1720 György Száraz, one of the confidants of the king, utilized the remaining and usable parts for the construction of a new aristocratic house. Later on the husband of his daughter, Julianna, started constructing a new building satisfactory to his wealth in 1743.

Corresponding to the High Baroque style, the front view of the castle has *a stressed middle part between the side wings surrounding the formal courtyard*. It is accentuated, as the main entrance accompanied by columns and above this the banqueting hall, the scene of social and musical events can be found. Decorated arms, statues and stone vases are increasing the luxury of *the main*

60

façade (60). The building follows the style of the castle in Gödöllő – described later – representing the type of construction named after Antal Grassalkovich, who established this concept throughout the Carpathian basin in the 18th century.

The communicating rooms are decorated with figural wall paintings and *Rococo stoves (59)*. Today the castle is a *museum presenting interiors from the Middle Ages up to the middle of the 19th century (58)*. There are suites of furniture for the bourgeois and the noble based on the collection of the Museum of the Applied Arts.

A rather civic and ecclesiastic face of the Baroque architecture can be noticed at the foot of Castle Hill, in *Víziváros*. Its main street is running parallel with the river and at its extension *two beautiful churches* were erected.

They both were constructed between 1740–60 and one of them was enlarged with a *monastery*. Their appearances are restrained, only decorated spires and some statues reflect the late-Baroque era but their interiors show all the luxury of the Rococo on the altars, pulpits and paintings.

The *nearer building* was in the possession *of the Franciscan friars* and *the farther* is the *parish-church* of the quarter *(61)*.

The *Franciscan church* was named after St. John of Capistrano fighting beside János Hunyadi in the battle of Belgrade in 1456 and having a decisive role in the successful defence. The followers of friar John originating from Capistrano nearby Rome constructed their monasteries in Bosnia and later on in Hungary. In the place of the Franciscans nursing nuns arrived from Vienna in 1785.

The high altar of the *St. Anne parish-church* is an excellent work of art on which, under the cupola reminding to an antique church, the child Maria, his parents Anne and Joachim, as well as Elisabeth can be seen. The church has guarded its Baroque style and reflects the quality of the ecclesiastic art of Buda in the Rococo era.

Close to the parish-church another Baroque monument, the *former 'White Cross' rest house* can be found. It was constructed around 1770 and within its walls theatre performances and balls were held *(62)*.

61

62

63

64

In the main street of Víziváros (Water Town) a *Turkish bath*, named after the family *Király*, can be found *(63)*. It was built by Musztafa Szokollu Pasha around 1570. After its name – 'Kakaskapu iliçe' (Cock Gate Thermal Bath), a town gate might have been standing in its neighbourhood. Its *polygonal pool* is located in the centre *under a huge cupola born by ogee arches*, and further smaller basins are placed in the corners with thermal waters of different degree. The exterior of the bath, the hierarchy of the cupolas reflect well its interior arrangement, while the stalactite vaults and arcades reveal the *sparkling solutions of the Ottoman architecture (64)*.

Upwards along the Danube there is a further Turkish monument. On *Rózsadomb* a small domed edifice and its saint area can be discovered, i.e. the *'Türbe' (burial-hill) of Gül baba*, named after a saint man, the Father of the Roses. A *picturesque small street (67)* of an atmosphere of the 19th century leads to the burial chapel erected by Mehmet Pasha of Buda between 1543–48. After 1686 a monastery was standing adjacent to the characteristic octagonal edifice of the *burial place (66)*, which was used by Jesuits as a vineyard chapel. Later on it became to a decorative element in a garden of a neo-Renaissance villa. The original *tomb of the Father of Roses (65)* is already irretraceable but the interior and the surrounding reflect well the atmosphere of the former Muslim world.

65

66

67

68

69

70

When the statute about Budapest was born *Óbuda* was the smallest, but the oldest administrative constituent including Aquincum, capital of Pannonia in the Roman Age.

The Hungarian chieftains also installed their seat here by using the ruins of the amphitheatres. Later a small settlement and then the church of the provostship and a royal fortress were constructed, in which King Béla III received Frederick Barbarossa in 1189. The terrible destruction by the Tartars ceased the golden ages in 1241. In the following century the Queen built up a convent for the Clares, then Sigismund of Luxembourg founded a university in Óbuda, as well.

After the Turkish era the *Zichy family* acquired the area: between 1746–57 they built a charming *palace on the Danube bank (72)* and an important *monastery for the Trinitarians (73)* on the hillside, which is actually a museum for the collection of the capital.

After 1872 Óbuda had been guarding its provincial character for a long time and still is reputed for its *entertainment*, too *(70)*. A fragment from this can be seen at the foot of the Árpád Bridge. The *Baroque complex of the parish-church and parsonage* (built up between 1744–49) enriched by statues and altars rises from the surrounding small houses *(68)*.

An other 'isle' reflecting Óbuda's past by Roman and medieval remains is the area around the 19th-century *Town Hall (69)*. All of a sudden, bronze statues are coming in front of us at an intimate square : *'Girls carrying umbrellas' (71) by Imre Varga*, the outstanding master of the plastic arts of the 20th century.

71

72

73

74

75

The limestone containing surface waters keep on creating a special world in the bowels of the mountains over millions of years. They shape not only *caverns*, but *drop stones* pending from the roof or growing upwards from the bottom of the cave and being slowly transformed into columns,as well. *The cave of Pál-völgy* was explored at the beginning of the 20th century then further sections became visible in a length of 13 km. The drop stones suggest several fantasy names to the rooms after their forms (Snow-White and the seven Dwarves), or the view coming into sight (Theatre, Devil's Kitchen, etc.). One of the famed formations may be found in the *Rope Ladder room* demonstrating well the development of the nature over millions of years *(74)*.

Thermal waters attracted people to develop the Roman town, *Aquincum*, in the 1st century A.D. The capital of the province Pannonia Inferior lived its golden age in the 2nd and 3rd centuries with 60,000 inhabitants. At first the legionary camp was built up at the foot of theÁrpád Bridge protected with bastions and water trenches to defend the crossing place from Barbarian's attacks.

Outside the camp the remains of villas, baths, and an early-Christian tomb chapel were found. The *military amphi-*

theatre (75) has been known ever since its construction around 150 A.D.

The *civic town* was established to the north of the camp. By the end of the 2nd century the town became the most important centre of the province, and within its walls the buildings followed the Roman standards. The Capitoline sanctuary, the curia – seat of the magistracy, the hall of justice and the basilica were located on the main square, the Forum. The market and meat hall, the public bath were placed in the centre and, at a distance of some hundred meters, another amphitheatre was built. The water of the neighbouring sources arrived here by a pipeline ('aquaductus') and was conducted further to the military town.

The magistrates and the inhabitants made efforts to establish circumstances equalling to those in Rome. This also applies to the air heating of houses, the frescoes, the decorative mosaics on the floors, or such simple articles for personal use, like the *'aquamanile'* beating the drum which can be seen in the *local museum (76)*.

After the fall of the empire the buildings remained in use, as stone quarry, either. In the Renaissance era the ruins were highly esteemed and excavations were made at the end of the 1700s, however, the systematic research in the civic town started in the 1880s, the results of which are exposed in the *garden of ancient ruins* and the *museum (77)*.

76

77

79

Upwards along the river the sights of the *Danube Bend* attract the visitors. The first station is *Szentendre* (together with Vác on the opposite riverside). The Pilis hills form the view and the silhouette of the town interlarded with church towers at the Danube side. On its hills rolling down to the river small houses, winding streets and small squares follow one another *(78, 79, 82)*.

Szentendre had an important role both in the Roman era and in the Middle Ages, but its actual appearance has been determined decisively by the sorrowful events at the end of the 17th century. In 1690 the town was populated with Serb refugees under the leadership of Arsenije Crnojević driven away by the Turks, and their tradesmen and merchants established a flourishing town here. They built several *churches* complying with the European Baroque-style in their appearances *(81)*, but the immoderation of the *Rococo dominate their interiors* with the traditional *iconostases* placed before the sanctuary *(80)*.

Later the artists frequented the town for its atmosphere, settled down, and numerous important works of the 20th-century fine art were realized here. Today its impressive streets, small restaurants, museums and peculiar churches offer interesting experience.

80

81

82

83

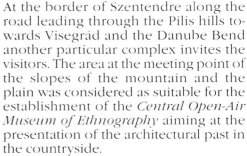

85

At the border of Szentendre along the road leading through the Pilis hills towards Visegrád and the Danube Bend another particular complex invites the visitors. The area at the meeting point of the slopes of the mountain and the plain was considered as suitable for the establishment of the *Central Open-Air Museum of Ethnography* aiming at the presentation of the architectural past in the countryside.

The houses, farm buildings and churches brought from different places were re-built here by preserving their original structural elements and guarding their original forms and the shape

84

of sites. The authentic memories of the Hungarian rural architecture in an environment almost similar to the places of origin illustrate duly the housing culture in the 18th and 19th centuries.

At first the complex presenting the region at the *upper section of the Tisza river* was established, which formerly abounded with forests. The *campanile* in its centre (carpentered in 1667) represents a masterpiece of the carpentry and is very charactertstic of the region.

A *Protestant church* (built in 1787) stands beside the wooden campanile, as most people there are Calvinists *(86)*. The interior of the church decorated with *painted wooden ceiling, carved choir, benches and pulpit* of the abundance of the Rococo met the demand of the lower nobles' congregation *(87)*.

Adjacent to the church and the belfry the characteristics of the rustic architecture of the poor can be observed on a *peasant house* with wooden structure and the high roof covered by wheat thatch. The house served as dwelling place for two families, in the first room the young, while in the one in the rear their parents lived, and between the two rooms was a kitchen *(84)*.

In the courtyard wattle maize shed, a specially formed draw well and a *dry mill* can be found *from Vámosoroszi*

(85). The word 'dry' shows that neither the water nor the wind, but horses were turning the millstones by going round in a circular tent.

In 1846, after four decades of operation a steam mill made the dry mill uneconomical. That's why its proprietor, the Protestant congregation transformed the mill to be suitable for pressing of oil containing seeds and this way it functioned almost further four decades.

The second complex is of the *'Kisalföld region' (83)*. Kisalföld is a plain in North Western Hungary abounding in rivers and good harvest. The crop had excellent market in the neighbouring towns: Győr, Pozsony, Sopron. Most houses there reflect well the prosperity of the economy, but modest ones can also be found there. The belfry in the centre was erected in 1855 by the Lutheran lower nobility.

This place is not only a museum, on holidays and weekends visitors may get acquaintance with the popular trades, music and dance. At such occasions the museum is also transformed, people are cooking, cutting, weaving, baking bred, singing and both the child and the adult can find some entertainment.

86

87

88

89

The Danube Bend is the most beautiful and diversified trench of the river. Here, between the cuddling Pilis and Börzsöny hills, the Danube becomes narrow to about 200 meters and breaks trough towards the plain then immediately falls apart to create the Szentendre Island.

Years one million ago the two mountains constituted a single chain and blocked up the course of the river. Due to the volcanic movements and the force of the water the mountain was split into two and opened a passage. Peaks of 300–600 meters high with deep valleys among them accompany the river. The Danube Bend became part of the Danube-Ipoly National Park for its rich flora, fauna and for the valuable monuments there.

On the right bank the Romans built up a protective line to control both the road along the riverside and the navigation, as well as against the Barbarians. One of the sights of this beautiful region is *Visegrád* with the *Citadel (88)* and the *Lower Fortress, a large donjon (89)*. These fortifications guarded the region, controlled the road from Buda to Esztergom, and the river, too. Both of them were erected in the second half of the 13th century against the renewed attacks of the Tartars, as it was proven, that only the fortresses of stone are able to resist. They were in the possession of the sovereigns until 1543, i.e. the date of the siege of the Turks.

Under the protection of the fortress the sovereigns of the Anjou dynasty constructed a palace in the international Gothic style. The beautiful complex became the home of the royal court at the time of Charles Robert and Louis I, the Great. Later on the king's household was moved to Buda and the *Palace of Visegrád* served as a summer residence.

After 1543 slow decay transformed the beautiful Gothic-Renaissance ensemble into ruins. In the 18th century German settlers used it as stone quarry, later waters run downhill from the mountains and covered it with earth to make it invisible for two hundred years. The first traces were found at the end of 1934 in suggesting that the remains of the disappeared palace – described in the deeds of the 15th and 16th centuries as so luxurious – were revealed. Following this, more and more fragments of the buildings became known, e.g. the *Hercules-fountain by Giovanni Dalmata* – educated on the Italian Renaissance principles – in the centre of the formal courtyard *(91)*. The *courtyard* itself looks like a Gothic cloister *(92)* topped off with a *Renaissance loggia*. The palace from King Matthias' period also presents this particular duality: as the *lion-adorned wall fountain (90)* from 1483 reflects, the ornaments of the Renaissance co-existed harmoniously with the works from previous periods.

90

91

92

94

95

Esztergom at the gate of the Danube Bend was the centre of the early Hungarian Kingdom. Around 971 Great Prince Géza set up his residence on the Fortress Hill, where our first King, Stephen – canonized saint – was born and crowned. The centre of the archbishopric was also built up on the Fortress Hill around 1010 with the cathedral and the palace. In 1198 King Béla III handed over the residence to the bishop and Esztergom became and remained as for today the centre of the Hungarian Christianity.

The *Neoclassical Basilica (93)* is the greatest and first rank cathedral in Hungary. The adjacent museum complex guards the restored *remains of the royal residence (98)* from the end of the 12th century, e.g. a detail of a *marble-inlaid armrest of a throne (96)*.

Prior to the Basilica, a cathedral was built on the site in honour of St. Adalbert, but during the sieges against the Turks it deteriorated and even its ruins were demolished, when the new church was erected. Only the *Renaissance sepulchral chapel* constructed in 1506 for Bishop Tamás Bakócz has preserved its brilliance *(95)*.

The archbishopric returned to the town in 1820: the Prince-Primate was aiming at establishing an imposing ecclesiastical centre here, from this plan only the cathedral, the prebendal and archiepiscopal palaces, furthermore the seminary were realized. József Hild, leader architect of the Neoclassical style created the plans of the

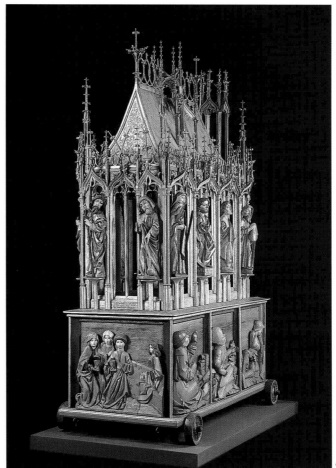

97

96

98

cathedral, which was consecrated in August 1856 in the presence of Emperor Francis Joseph and accompanied with the performance of the Mess composed by Ferenc Liszt for this occasion. The relieves, statues and paintings were prepared by Italian, German, Austrian and Hungarian sculptors and painters. *Michelangelo Grigoletti painted the reproduction of Assunta* by Tiziano, of which the original can be seen in the Frari Church in Venice, the *paintings by Ludwig Moralt* for the high altar and *in the cupola* illustrate the Fathers of the church *(94)*.

A further pride of the town is the *Christian Museum* with numerous brilliant works of the Hungarian and foreign ecclesiastical art of the Middle Ages and the later centuries, like this Gothic *'Holy Sepulchre' coffin (97)* carved in the second half of the 1500s.

Margaret Island gained its today's form in the mid-19th century; formerly there were four small isles in its place. It was called also the Island of Rabbits, the Maiden's Island by the Turks and later on, becoming in the palatines' proprietorship, Palatinus Island. The island takes its name after Béla IV's daughter, Princess St. Margaret.

In the middle of the medieval period a *monastery* for Premonstratensian friars and a *convent* for Dominican nuns were established here and Margaret lived here,too. Her saint life consecrated her tomb to a place of pilgrimage. The buildings were deteriorated and the archaeological excavations explored the *convent's remains* between the two World Wars *(100)*. The monastery was also revealed and from among its remains the St. Michael chapel was restored.

Two famous *swimming pools (102)* were established on the is-

99

100

101

102

103

land using its thermal waters discovered in 1866.

Beside its past, the island is famous for its collection of special
trees. In 1790, when Archduke
Alexander Leopold took the island
in his possession, he started re-
shaping it on the model of the park
of the Schönbrunn Palace. Charles
Louis and palatine Joseph followed his efforts. Later on the island became to the proprietorship
of the capital and by the plantation
of several thousand special trees
and shrubs a *park collecting rare
plants* was born *(104)*.

Not only a park can be found
here, but a rose-garden, a *water-
fall (103)*, a *rock garden (99)* and
a *music-fountain (101)*, as well.

Among the edifices and statues
special trees – limes, Japanese aca-
cias, willows, pines, black walnut-
trees, maples, etc. – and different
superior shrubs are flourishing.

104

The *northern part of the Inner Town* on the left Danube bank stretches from the Chain Bridge to the Margaret Bridge. In the bottom of the picture the first section of Andrássy Avenue linking the Inner Town with City Park (Városliget) is presented with the Opera House accompanied by neo-Renaissance palaces. This view is due to two urban development plans: the Embellishment Plan laid down in 1805 for shaping up the embankments and their surroundings, then the realization of the system of boulevards and avenues commenced in the 1870s.

From the summer 2002 Andrássy Avenue also appears in the World Heritage Register with the underground electric train, the first tube in the continent realized in 1896.

The area along the Danube is the centre of the public administration, the financial and commercial life, and the *Basilica*, the second rank cathedral in the Esztergom-Budapest main diocese named after King St. Stephen, was also erected here in the second half of the 19th century *(106)*.

After 1867, the date of the Compromise with the Habsburg dynasty the capital became to a metropolis. The *Parliament building (105)* with the session-rooms for the Lower and Upper House and the cupola connecting the two wings is a primary symbol of the state independence. The building, especially its view from the Danube is a most characteristic element of Budapest. At the time of its construction the area of Hungary was substantially larger – the members of the Parliament came from 63 counties to the Lower House in spite of 19 counties as today. The Prime Minister and his assistance also work here and the parade ground before the building is the place of state ceremonies. One of the most memorable event of the recent past was the announcement of the new state form, the Hungarian Republic on 23rd October 1989, when Hungary committed itself to the course of the democracy desired for such a long time.

105

107

When the concept of an almost independent and dual state was outlined, the capital was lacking of a building for the bicameral Parliament. As a temporary solution the sessions of the Upper House were held in the Hungarian National Museum and the deputies held the sessions in a building erected in rush for this purpose. The building constructed in a few months and finished in the spring of 1866, was a transitive solution, because everybody knew that the *new Parliament (105)* would have been built at the northern unloading dock for timber. However, the works began as late as in 1885. The architect, winner at the competition, Imre Steindl faced with many difficulties, since he had to plan the foundations for a building of a length of 300 meters and of a height of almost 100 meters at the cupola on the alluvial deposit of the Danube.

The designer having excellent knowledge of the medieval and especially the *Gothic architecture* made this style to *dominate* the Parliament for two reasons. This was the style applied on the building of the English Parliament and this style characterized the constructions of Sigismund and Matthias in the 15th century, in the brilliant decades of the Hungarian Middle Ages. If, however, the mass and silhouette of the building

108

109

are examined more precisely, marks of the Baroque would also be revealed in the appearance of the session rooms. This duality continues in the interior of the building.

The elegant and majestic *main staircase (108)* and mainly its vaults reflect the Baroque style, the style of the Hungarian revival after the Turkish destruction, and this characterizes also the hall under the cupola. Whereas the *supporting structures* – the columns, arcades, retaining pillars, etc. – are medieval-like everywhere in the session rooms, corridors, and even in the central hall *(107, 109), the vaults,* however, can be traced back to the archetype style of the 18th century *(108, 109)*.

The architectural elegance is combined with the richness of the artistic works and the abundance of the noble materials. Everything is coloured and full of movement. Here are kings standing under laced stone towers, and there *figures indicating trades (110)* can be seen. At other places arms or historical paintings are coming in our sight, while somewhere else the decorative ornamental painting dominates.

In this luxury from the end of the 19th century the symbols of the statehood: *the Holy Crown, the orb and the sceptre* are guarded *(107, 111)*.

110

111

112

113

114

115

116

In Kossuth Square – in addition to the Parliament – other important buildings stand, like the most decorative *Hungarian Museum of Ethnography* constructed at the end of the 1900s by Alajos Hauszmann, who reconstructed the Royal Palace, too. The main façade is ornamented with works by excellent sculptors and the decorative staircase with frescoes by Károly Lotz. The building of the monumental stream of the Historicity was originally the seat of the Supreme Court. The elegant, solemn and pompous use of the Renaissance and Baroque elements, as well as noble materials is worthy of the original functions *(116)*.

Several statues enhance the solemnity of the square. The *equestrian statue of Ferenc Rákóczi II* reminds on the war of independence against the Habsburgs from 1703 *(112)*, to which the *figure of Lajos Kossuth*, leader of the fight for freedom in 1848–49 is facing *(114)*, and the small square giving on the Parliament is decorated with the *statue of Imre Nagy*, the martyr Prime Minister of the revolution in 1956 *(117)*. In its neighbourhood the *sanctuary lamp* on a decorated pedestal remembers *Count Lajos Batthyány*, the first responsible Prime Minister executed to death in 1849 *(115)*.

Opposite to the neo-Renaissance seat of the Hungarian Academy of Sciences the *statue of Count István Széchenyi* stands at the abutment of the Chain Bridge *(113)*. Széchenyi was the mediator of the modernization of the country from the 1830s, supported on his own income the establishment of the Hungarian Society of Scientists, organized and directed the construction of the Chain Bridge, the first permanent connection crossing the Danube in Hungary.

117

118

119

120

Most of the buildings in the Inner Town and the adjoining Leopold Town are dwelling houses and several of them were built in the first half of the 1800s in the Neoclassical style. Others give fine examples of the Romanticism imitating medieval elements, but the majority was constructed in the last trimester of the 19th and at the beginning of the 20th century.

As for the ecclesiastical buildings, the most important ones are the parish-church, the Baroque monasteries of the Paulines, the single religious order founded by Hungarians, and the Franciscans, the convent of the Mary Ward's nuns, and the Greek Orthodox churches.

The Inner Town has been the centre of the public administration, trade and financial affairs for a long time illustrated by the decorative *window by Miksa Róth* in the staircase *(120)* and the *board room (119)* of the *National Bank of Hungary*, or by the *Stock Exchange Palace* figured on the upper part in the aerial photo *(121)*.

The *very special bank building (121)* differs from the ostentatious style of the age and represents the individual and *characteristically Hungarian course of the Secession*. Its designer, *Ödön Lechner* gave up imitating the Historic styles and in 1901 formed façades and roofs with abundant places for decorations made of glazed ceramics with motives of the popular art. This appears in the *interior spaces and staircases*, too *(118)*.

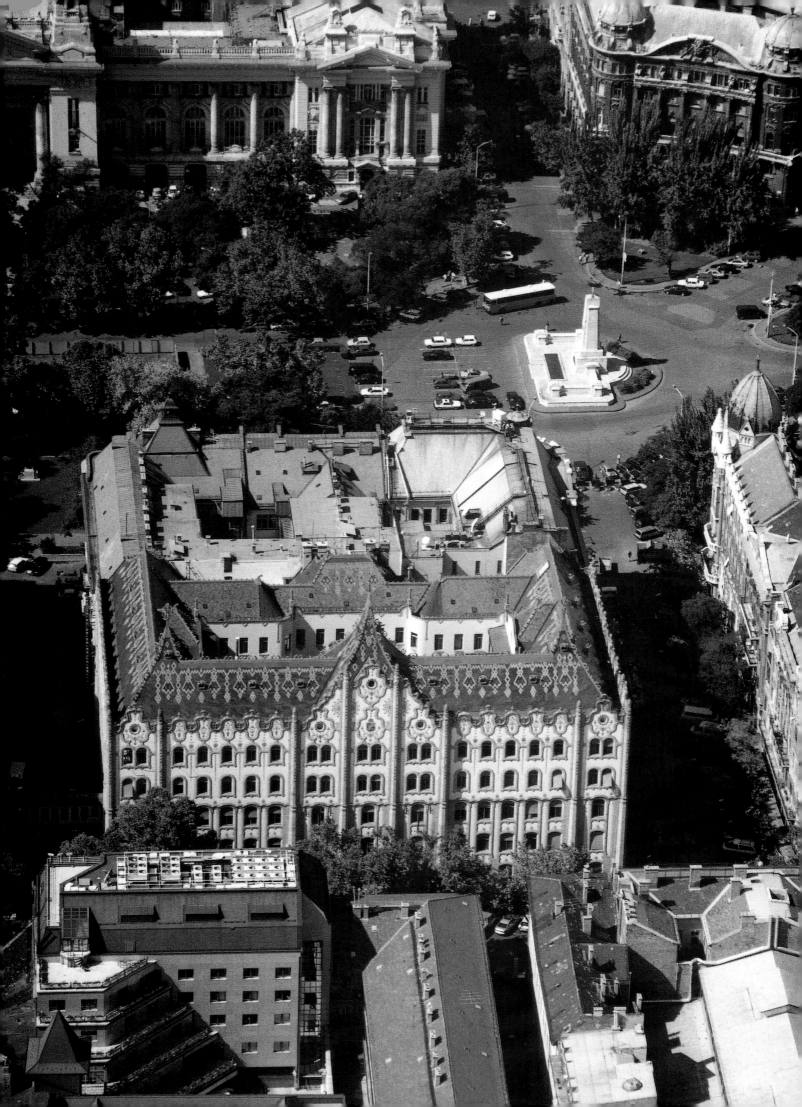

The northern part of the Inner Town is called Lipótváros after the Habsburg sovereign, Leopold approving the Embellishment Plan. Farther from the river, this area was still unbuilt in the first half of the 19th century and a parish-church was erected here.

The construction started in 1851 according to the Neoclassical plans by József Hild, the most popular master of Pest. The interior was modelled after the St. Peter Basilica in Rome and the church of the Invalids in Paris, the domed central part surrounded by eight squares ranked among the classical solutions. After the death of Hild, in 1867 Miklós Ybl took over the planning, and the construction works started anew with removing debris – the cupola collapsed. After a fundamental re-planning, the

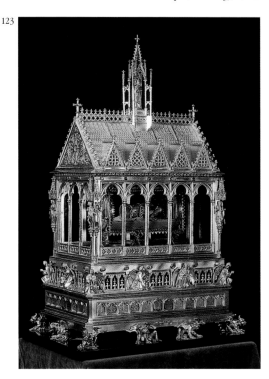

neo-Renaissance cathedral, the *Basilica (122)* was completed in 1905. At first its name was taken from St. Leopold, the protective saint of the royal house, but since 1897 its eponym has been King St. Stephen.

The richness of the church is due to the excellent works of the sculptors and painters of the age *(124)*. The *high altar* is decorated with the *statue of King St. Stephen* with the orb in his left hand and the patriarchal cross in his right, and on the top of the baldachin an angel is holding the Holy Crown *(125)*. Relieves and the Virgin Mary altar painting on the apse wall illustrate the merits of the saint king. The *reliquary* guarding the *mummified right hand* of King St. Stephen *(123)* is being kept here in an individual chapel.

The Inner Town is structured by smaller and larger squares. Their development was relating to the market places within the town walls, for example in 1812 Vörösmarty Square was the market in 'Theátrom Platz'. In Leopold Town the formation of the larger squares is due to comprehensive development plans. As for Liberty Square, the 'New Edifice', purpose-built for barracks and prison was demolished and in place of that, dwelling-houses, public buildings and squares were formed.

In Pest surrounded by medieval walls the markets were held in the streets, which disturbed the inhabitants. In 1789 the magistracy made a decision on mar-

126

128

127

king out an area at the border of the town for this purpose and in 1790 the *Market Place* (in Erzsébet Square) was opened bearing later expressive names depending on its actual duties. It was also named after the German Theatre, then it was 'Promenaden Platz', later on it received the name of *Queen Elisabeth*, the spouse of Francis Joseph, engaged towards the Hungarians (1858). Further on it was Stalin Square, and from his death to 1990 the place took its name after Friedrich Engels. The square was given back its ancient name after the change of the political system.

The names changed and the sights altered, as well. There are *houses* from the first half *of the 19th century* and houses with windows recalling me-dieval forms *(126)*. From a *doorway* a pretty young girl *(128)* regards us.

In the centre of the square the *Danubius fountain*, the common work of the well-known Miklós Ybl and the sculptor, Leó Feszler can be seen from 1883 *(127)*. The three women are the symbols of the rivers Tisza, Dráva and Száva, and the martial man standing uppermost personifies the Danube collecting these waters.

Two modern hotels were constructed on the square, one of them is the *Kempinski Hotel Corvinus (129)*.

Elisabeth Square is followed by Madách Square connected by a *small square* – the cabbage market in the 18th century – *named after Ferenc Deák*, promoter of the Compromise of 1867. In the neighbouring Invalids' Palace a grenadier regiment was garrisoned from 1783. The Emperor's order of 1787 declared religious tolerance and made it possible for the *Evangelic* soldiers and *Lutheran* citizens of Pest and its environs to erect a church, but only outside the town walls. An oratory and the vicarage were built up first, later on the *church* itself with the direction of the leading personality of the Neoclassical architecture, *Mihály Pollack (130)*. In support of Protestant aristocrats the church was canonized in 1811 at Pentecost. The religious services were done in German, Slovakian and Hungarian languages following the composition of the congregation. A museum adjacent to the church demonstrates the past of the Hungarian evangelicalism.

129

130

131

132

A large number of Jewish lived in the medieval capital, Buda and researchers discovered their synagogue in a civic house in the northern part of the Castle District. The Jewish community in Pest was estab-lished relatively late, and elected its first rabbi in 1796.

As fast the growing Pest-Buda became the industrial and commercial centre of the country, as rapidly the number and prosperity of the Jewish increased. During the 1850s a request by the Jewry of 30,000 arose for building up a synagogue on a purchased plot outside the town walls. Ludwig Förster, architect of the great synagogue in Vienna, was commissioned with the works, and due to his excellent organization, *the largest synagogue in the Continent* was completed between 1854–59 *(131)*.

The edifice differs from the traditional ones not only with its dimensions and galleries, but also *with placing the Holy Ark* at the rear of the longitudinal axis, similarly to catholic churches *(132)*. It was a novelty to apply façade towers aiming at accentuating the church-like appearance. The particular and oriental-like decoration of the building created a school. The 'Moresque' style fitted in well with the Romanticism: it was not the past, but the remote world that inspired Förster. At the adjacent museum building there is a memorial place, too: *'The weeping willow' by Imre Varga* keeps bending here with the names of the holocaust's martyrs on its leaves *(133)*.

133

134

At the beginning of the 19th century both the common interests and the bourgeois mentality required public museums for the collections in place of the private ones being closed from the public eyes. The Glyptothek in Munich, the British Museum in London, or the Altes Museum in Berlin were established this way.

The issue of the *National Museum* was the indication of increasing social consciousness and the aspiration for independence: consequently, it failed to meet the satisfaction of the court ruling from Vienna. In 1802 *Ferenc Széchényi* – the father of István Széchenyi, called 'the greatest Hungarian' – *donated his collection and library* to the people of the country. Though, a number of obstacles had to be overcome until 1837, when the construction could start on basis of the *plans by Mihály Pollack (134)*.

In 1838 a glacial flood devastated Pest-Buda by destroying more than the half of the houses. It is understandable: the first task was the reconstruction and hardly any vigour left to continue on building the museum. The plans were simplified, noble materials, as well as a part of the works of art to be purchased had to be omitted. The museum opened in 1846, but the formation of the neo-Renaissance main staircase could take place only at the end of the 1860s, praising the work of Miklós Ybl. The paintings for the ceiling by Mór Than and Károly Lotz – the allegoric figures of Imagination, Enthusiasm, Observation, Tradition, and Inspiration – were completed afterwards. Onto the lateral walls stories were depicted about the

135

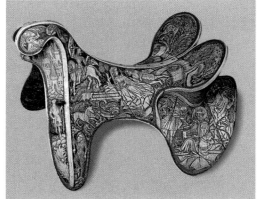

136

Hungarian nation's past : the Hungarian conquest, the admission and propagation of the Christianity, the foundation of schools, the stations of material and spiritual rise and the foundation of the National Museum. The route from the colonnade through the row of adjoining spaces of the entrance hall, the main staircase and the ceremonial hall became elegant and solemn.

In front of the *main façade (134)* a figural composition by Alajos Strobl commemorates János Arany, one of the stars of the Hungarian poetry in the 19th century. Under the statue of the sitting poet of the trilogy 'Toldi', his two protagonists personify the epic poem (Miklós Toldi) and the popular poetry (Piroska Rozgonyi). The monument to the poet, deceased 11 years before, was unveiled in 1893.

The Museum of Fine Arts and the Museum of Applied Arts were separated from the National Museum and became independent collections, and the National Library was also working here for a long time.

Nowadays on permanent expositions are displayed e.g. *the cope, belonging to the Coronation Insignia prepared in 1031 under surveillance by the Queen (138)*, and one of the most beautiful souvenirs from the Hungarian past, a decorated *sabretache plate* to protect the most important belongigngs of equestrians *(135)*, a wonderful *horn saddle* carved at the beginning of the 1400s from the court of Sigismund (136) and, finally, a *throne carpet* decorated with the royal arms from the end of the 15th century *(137)*.

Rows of elegant palaces surround the museum and its beautiful garden. They were built mostly for aristocrats in the 19th century. One of them is housing the German University 'Count Gyula Andrássy' and the ancient House of Commons is used by the Institute of Italian Culture.

137

138

139

In the Inner Town surrounded by medieval walls some palaces were also erected for aristocrats, e.g. the *Károlyi palace* was constructed in the early 1830s by using of former buildings, following the plans of the Viennese Anton Riegl and Henrik Koch. A beautiful garden has belonged to the palace, which is a *public park today (142),* and the palace itself became the *Museum of Literature.*

Farther the *University Church's* towers appeare. The church was constructed for the Pauline friars. The order funtioned from 1309 and followed the rules of St. Augustin. Two hundred years later they had 63 houses in the country and established the monas-tery becoming the place of pilgrimage in Czestochowa, Poland.

The Turks ravaged their mother monastery located in the Buda Hills, where the mortal remains of the eponymous Hermit St. Paul of Thebe were guarded.

After their return, the friars received a plot in Pest for the construction of a new church and monastery . The complex was built up in 1742, but its altars and frescoes were completed only afterwards. Emperor Joseph II suppressed all monastic orders and gave the opportunity to function only for those, which undertook useful public activity. Finally, in 1805, the Paulines' church and friary were handed over to the central seminary of the Catholic Church and its name, 'University Church' derives from here.

140

141

142

The wood sculptor friars living in the monasteries carved the wonderful *library* of their friary in Pest *(139)* and, among others, the *benches of the church (143)* decorated with the scenes from the life of St. Paul.

In 1686, when the Turks were expelled, Pest and Buda were destroyed into ruins and they had to be inhabited anew. Hungarians, Germans and Slovaks arrived here and South Slavs, first of all the Serbs represented a special colour among the settlers. They were rather town-dwellers dealing with commerce or handicraft. The Habsburgs granted them rights for free exercise of their religion, construction of church, election of the bishop, as well as considerable self-governing rights. Due to the separation, traditions and privileges the community lived a succesful life.

In Pest the *Serbs* made their *Church* built by local masters, therefore it is resembling to a catholic church in its appearance and the architectural details of the interior *(140)*.

As for the furniture and the paintings, they differ completely: a picture wall separates the sanctuary from the place for the believers, men were sitting separately from women. The *iconostas* differs only in respect of the pictures representing traditional orthodox style and themes *(141)*.

The church was built up for 1750, its furniture was made by Mihajlo Janić Serb carver and the pictures were painted later on by Károly Sterio originating from Greece.

143

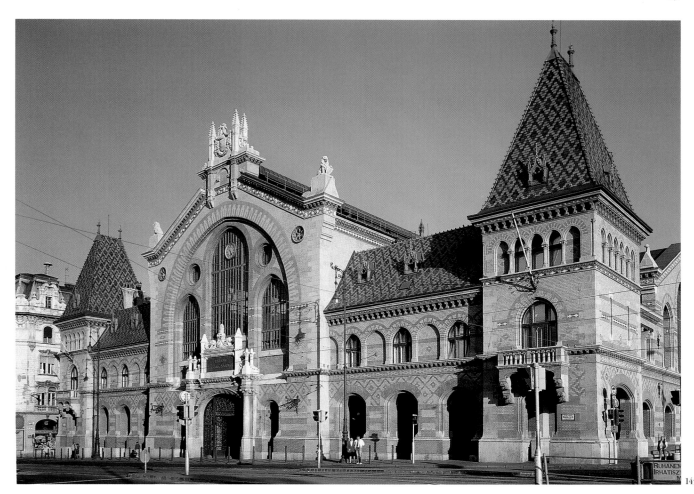

145

146

Around 1890 the number of the inhabitants in Budapest was already more than half a million and the capital possessed 44 markets – without water supply. The most favourable market place was at the Danube bank. As for the public health and hygiene, the situation was deteriorating more and more and illness bearer rodents occurred around the rubbish-shoot. An overall market hall system was required to change this situation, therefore in 1890 the municipal councillors decided to construct the central market hall and eight regional ones for the districts.

Samu Pecz, professor of the Technical University, planned the *central market hall* at the beginning of 1894. The environment, e.g. the Main Customs House by Miklós Ybl, required a historical appearance. Pecz chose a solution from the Middle Ages, as if he had constructed a *fortress of trade* (145). He applied metal structure for the interior in order to achieve easily accessible and more visible space connections. The market hall looks *like a small town* with main and cross-streets (144) with an immense cellar, where the goods were transported formerly by railway and ships. The central market hall opened in 1897 is a most important shop for food (146) in the capital and a *tourist spectacle*, too.

147

The *Museum of Applied Arts* is one of the most spectacular buildings in Budapest. The name of its designer, Ödön Lechner, has already been learnt in connection with the building adjoining to the National Bank (121).

Corresponding to the tradition of the age, the building was used not only as a museum, but a school of industrial arts, as well. The exterior of the edifice, the high cupola visible from farther points of the town, the coloured roofing and the floral-patterned decorative elements attract the visitors. There is a vivid world there: especially an exciting and unusual intersection connecting the two storeys of the foyer, particular forms of the parapets and apertures, and finally the *huge glass-hall* carried by lace like steel structure *(147)*. The view of the hall is definitely bizarre, but it should be considered that the Historicity was already ruling there for three decades and Lechner would have made it forgotten. This work provoked fierce debates in 1896, but the literature of the architecture now ranks Lechner's art equal to that of Gaudí, the Spanish architect.

In 1872 the Parliament provided an amount for purchasing the first pieces of the collection, which by now has become extremely rich in ancient Hungarian embroideries, French, Netherlandish and *Oriental carpets (148), European glass and ceramic works (150)*, as well as *goldsmith's works of Nuremberg (151)*, Augsburg and *Hungary (149)*.

148

149

150

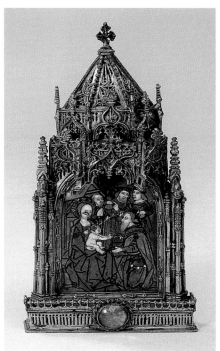

151

152

153

In the *neighbourhood of the National Museum* aristocratic palaces were erected for the Károlyi, Esterházy, Festetics families. It was a magnates' quarter and those, having no place neighbouring the museum made efforts to stay as close as possible. For this reason the *Wenckheim* family, successful in the business life, built up their *neo-Rococo palace* in 1887 *(152)*, functioning as *public library* today.

Budapest, born in 1872, started developing rapidly involving the area along Nagykörút ('the Grand Boulevard') *Elisabeth (Erzsébet)*, *Theresa (Teréz)* and *Joseph (József) towns*. Of course, 'towns' here mean districts famous for their theatres, forming the centre of the cultural life of the capital together with the cafés, the homes of the literal life. Their parish-churches from the 19th century are of great importance, too.

The *New York Café (153)* was established on the ground-floor of an insurance company's building in 1894. Its interiors in the neo-Baroque style attracted employees working for the neighbouring publishing houses or editor's offices, as well as writers and artists frequenting the theatres. In this really beautiful environment not only the service was eminent, but at their customary tables the regular guests received paper, ink and credit, as well. The New York Café lived its flourishing period during one and a half decades before the World War I.

Theresa Town takes its name from Empress Maria Theresa, perhaps the best-known Habsburg sovereign in the 18th century.

The most remarkable edifices in the quarter are the row of palaces in Andrássy Avenue, the Opera House and the *Academy of Music*, the two pillars of the musical life in the capital. The Academy named after Ferenc Liszt includes not only a concert hall for 1,200 persons, but also the University of Music.

The *edifice* represents a particular work in the late-Historical style, because on its *façade (155)* the characteristics of the 19th century and the beginning of the 20th century are still mixed, but as for its *interior*, the *Secession* becomes dominant *(156)*.

A really inspiring picture, *'The source of the arts'* by *Aladár Körösfői-Kriesch (154)*, with its several figures, painted in lively colours and gold appeals to the audience.

154

155

156

When the capital was born the view of Pest, with the exception of the Inner Town was quite untidy, whereas the rapid industrialization and the transformation into a capital city attracted a number of people from the provinces, and a more demanding layer of society also appeared, striving for purchasing a house or at least an elegant flat and to enjoy the social life. These requirements needed enough room and were served by an international invitation to tender in 1871, the result of which was the order of the present road system of the capital, as

157

159

158

compared to that of Paris, sometimes. A double boulevard system was developed around the established City and Leopold town, marking at the same time the places for the new Danube bridges. Small and Great Boulevards were broken through by avenues towards the already existing main country road system showing the route to Upper North Hungary, the eastern part of the country, the Great Hungarian Plain, as well as the southern area.

However, the role of *Andrássy Avenue*, registered in the World Heritage Sites was different: it has connected the centre to the largest green area of Pest, Városliget (City Park), this immense English garden. The avenue was formed accordingly: the façade of the *first house* looks like a gate with the *figure of Hermes on its gable (157)*. From here the avenue runs up to the first octagonal square, Oktogon. To obtain a better view of the Opera House, only one arcaded house was built in this section, the *Drechsler palace (158)* on the opposite side, by forming a smaller square in front of the most beautiful edifice in Andrássy Avenue.

Beyond Oktogon three parallel carriageways are running to the next octagonal square, the outer ones used to serve equestrians. At this place the closed, unbroken row of buildings ends, and the road runs on toward the park between loose and spacious rows of villas.

An attraction of the avenue is the underground railway, which has been the first electric tube in the continent. The management of the capital decided to realize this expensive and more complicated solution, because the traffic on the surface would have disturbed the view of the palace row and the calm of the people living there.

The row of imposing houses is embellished not only with architectural elements, but also with *sculptures* and *graffiti* carved out from the plaster layers *(159)*. In the *cross street* named also 'Broadway of Pest' the *façades of buildings* were formed with the similar fineness *(160)*. When popping in them *glazed windows in the Secession style (Ernst Museum: József Rippl-Rónai – 161)* or *interiors* from the past come into view *(Post Museum – 162)*.

161

160

162

163

164

The *Opera House (163)* is the best work of *Miklós Ybl* and of the architecture in the Carpathian basin at the end of the 19th century.

The architect, who studied in Italy had masters like Mihály Pollack (the architect of the National Museum) and Henrich Koch, designer of the Károlyi Palace in Fót. The first, still Romantic work by Ybl was the crypt topped with a magnificent parish-church for the count's family. Then a most brilliant career set out.

The request for a music-theatre in Pest had already arisen in the 1870s and the Opera House was realized quickly – by September 1884.

Ybl had to adjust the plans to fortunate and sometimes disadvantageous conditions. The architectural environment and the avenue itself were already of metropolitan dimensions and elegance, but the site was considerably narrow and deep. Due to these facts, all that was necessary for the guests – the main entrance, the foyer and the auditorium

165

166

– were located at the Avenue, and all else was placed at the rear of the plot. The *roof of the building (163)* was determined by the requirements of the limited height: that's why the stage and the auditorium were put under the *mansard roof,* while the lounge, the staircase and the foyer were pulled back under a modest one.

The adjustment of the environment-friendly shaped edifice to the avenue is facilitated by the fretwork of the neo-Renaissance façades, by stressing of the horizontal pieces, and in completion of all these, by the means of the fine arts.

The interior and the *main staircase (166)* were constructed from articulated elments of the Renaissance. The *foyer (164)* and the *auditorium (165)* became such an environment, that is worthy of the music by application of noble materials and ornaments, like the painting above the auditorium *by Károly Lotz, 'The apotheosis of the music'.*

On arriving at City Park Andrássy Avenue leads first into the square of an impressive composition. This is Heroes' Square, in its centre with the *monument commemorating the millennium of the Hungarian conquest in 896 (170)*. Uppermost on a high column an *angel* stands *with the symbols of the statehood* of more than one thousand years: the Holy Crown in his right hand and rises high the apostolic double cross with his left hand, as a memory of the Christianity *(171)*.

On the base of the column equestrian statues of the conquering tribes' chieftains stand and, as closing of the composition, sculptures of kings, palatines and governors are placed in the openings of the colonnade. The construction of the monument started in 1896, and most of the statues were created by György Zala.

Important public buildings surround the monument: on the right side the *Exhibition Hall*, on the left side the *Museum of Fine Arts* appeare. Their gates with the portico were borrowed from the Greek architecture.

The enactment commemorating the Hungarian conquest aimed at influencing mainly the culture and the education. The *Museum of Fine*

167

168

169

Arts was born in this spirit by the inspiration of the Kunsthistorisches Museum (1892) of Vienna. The building was completed in 1906 after the plans of Albert Schickedanz influenced by the ancient Greek architecture. To recall the past the reproduction of the Olympic Zeus Temple's pediment was used as tympanum, while inside the Renaissance, more precisely the cinquecento was the inspiring style. Elegance and generosity feature all communal spaces.

The paintings and statues were put together from several private collections, from materials of the Royal Palace of Buda and from regular purchases. The Egyptian collection has been developed from the results of excavations by our archaeologists over the past decades.

The museum has an extremely rich *collection of Spanish (El Greco – 167)* and *Italian* works of art *(equestrian statue by Leonardo da Vinci* or his circle *– 168)*, but the collection of *Greek vases (Grimani pitcher – 169)* and unique graphics from the Renaissance age until almost our days are also remarkable.

As all serious museums, the Museum of Fine Arts also receives foreign exhibitions. Therefore it is not enough to get acquainted with the permanent exhibitions, but also recommended to frequently get in here, some surprises might always be found.

On *the opposite bank of the lake* an interesting *group of buildings* can be discovered. It was built also at the time of the millennium and composed of buildings' reproductions from different periods. There is a chapel similar to the Romanesque Church of Ják from the 13th-century architecture and next to it stands 'the tower of torture' – as it is called popularly. The reproduction of the Castle of Vajdahunyad in Transylvania is the wing with tower and bastion looking on the lake, and the adjoining group of domed buildings is composed of the relics of our secular Baroque architecture and Renaissance ornaments from Upper Northern Hungary. The group of buildings called in the everyday language 'Castle of Vajdahunyad' is the *Museum of Agriculture (170)*.

172

The Park enriches the sights with one more museum, the Hungarian Transport Museum displaying among others the world's first hijacked aeroplane.

In the Park – also called popularly 'a Liget' ('the Bosky') – there is the Metropolitan Zoo, too. The idea of it, supported by the Society of Academicians, arose already in 1840, and it was opened in 1866 with almost six hundred animals, among them with 35 races donated by the Imperial couple. The Zoo deteriorated slowly because of financial reasons, but was saved finally by the Capital. In 1912 the *Metropolitan Zoo and Plant Garden* was re-opened with a new group of buildings, which is by now the home of 3,000 animals.

When the Zoo was built, its designers wanted to keep the animals in houses reminding of their place of birth, but where it was not possible, the buildings reflected a special stream of the Secession stemming from the rural architecture. Kornél Neuschloss planned an *oriental-like building* with cupola *for the elephants*, even placed a minaret beside it *(173)*. Tough, the Hungarian Secession trickles in with its stylised decoration in the cupola and on the enamelled ceramic elements.

In the *Amusement Park* neighbouring the Zoo, the *Roundabout* keeps on turning with its trumpeter-angels and black and white horses since 1906.

173

174

The 'Bosky' had been popular among the showmen for a long time, and the citizens flooded the park on Sundays. There was an entertainment quarter there during the Millennium Exhibition in 1896 named Ancient Buda Castle, but it rather reminded of an oriental bazaar made of wood or papier-mâché. After its demolition the neo-Rococo hall of the *Round-about (172)* was erected, which is by now *the only existing element of the old so-called English Park*.

The *Europa Nostra*, the greatest European organization for the heritage protection considered exemplary and *rewarded* the renovation of *the Elephant House and the Roundabout Building*.

Thermal waters keep on working in the *Széchenyi Thermal Bath*. The spring was opened up in 1876: the 76°C water comes to the surface from a depth of 1256 meters.

At first the *medicinal part*, the domed neo-Renaissance building, was completed in 1913, then about ten years later the *arched building serving the leisure time* opened for the public *(174, 175)*.

175

176

177

The *Royal Palace Museum* is the pride of Gödöllő, one of the small towns in the hilly country at the Cserhát Mountains.

The palace complex was taking shape over one and a half-century following the failure of the war of independence in 1711. In the monarchy ruled by the Habsburgs beside the aristocracy a new leading class sprang up recruited partly from the new proprietors of the recaptured regions and partly from the middle-noble persons being loyal to the royal court. Antal Grassalkovich, belonging to the latter, represented the royal court in Hungary since 1724. Elevated to count in 1743, Antal I formed vast estates from his skilfully acquired possessions.

The construction of the Palace started in 1735, and one and a half decade later the main building and the connecting twin-double-wings were completed, and a chapel was built into the domed part on the right side *(178)*.

The red marble balcony of the main façade followed the model of Schönbrunn near Vienna, the double-dome and the gold-and-white-banqueting-hall took the Royal

178

179

Palace of Buda as example. Antal II, elevated already to prince, placed a theatre in the left wing, and his son replaced the French park with an English landscape garden.

In 867 Francis Joseph I was crowned to Hungary's king and, as sovereign, he chose the Palace of Gödöllő for summer residence. The series of rooms leading to the left from the ceremonial hall were reserved for the monarch, on the opposite side – including the former suite of Maria Theresa – Queen Elisabeth – 'Sisi'– lived. Out of the 103 rooms 63 were for the staff use.

Between the two world wars the governor, Miklós Horthy also used it as summer residence. After 1945, when the Red Army possessed the annexes, similarly to other Hungarian palaces Gödöllő had a tragic and devastating fate. The major part of the main building became social care home, only the chapel maintained its original function and thus, its furniture survived, too.

The palace has been transformed into museum. At first the royal suites were provided with furniture – the *study of Francis Joseph (176), the reception room (177) and the dressing room of Queen Elizabeth (179).*

In the Inner Town gardens were
scattered along the town wall for a
long time mainly for tactical reasons. In case of attack defenders
could deploy more easily for the
defence, the attacker could not
burn up the area behind them.
This was the situation during the
Middle Ages and when Pest was relieved from the Turks, both demolished and empty areas were avail-
able for the town. The idea of en-
suring proper accommodation,
health and religious help to the
wounded and disabled men of the
war emerged at that time.

In 1716, the foundations of the
House of Invalids were laid down.
Anton Erhardt Martinelli from Vienna planned the early-Baroque
building *(184)*, which houses the
Office of the Mayor nowadays. The
relieves decorating the gates were
completed in 1735 and commemo-

180

181

182

rate the establisment, Emperor
Charles III and the victorious com-
mander, Eugene of Savoy.

The Neoclassical Pest County
Hall standing at the end of the
street was built in 1841.

The *Baroque Temple* and the
monastery *of the Servite's order*
were built up in the neighbourhood and were completed in 1732
with particularly beautiful furniture. The Baroque style can be observed both outside and inside,
even on the *high altar (182)*. However, the façade of the church overlooking Szervita Square was built
almost 150 years later, in 1871,
from the donations of affluent citizens. The high altar from 1740
shows St. Anne and her accompa-
nying-saints: St. Stephen and St.
Ladislas (Hungarian kings), St.
Joseph and St. John the Baptist.

There are *remarkable houses at Szervita Square*. One of them recalls the spirit of the 1870s. Next to it *a former bank house* stands from the 1910s and represents the traditional harsh '*Jugendstil*' manner, while the building to the right is the *messenger of the modern architecture (183)*.

Another smallish square is situated at the meeting point of three streets alongside the House of Invalids. The decoration here is the *Danaids' Well*.

The two bronze figures show the punishment of the husband-killer daughters of King Danaus – they must carry water in bottomless vessels forever *(180)*. Ferenc Sidló, who studied in Munich and Rome, modelled the figures of the well in 1933.

Only a few *civic houses of Pest* have remained from the end *of the 18ᵗʰ and the early-19ᵗʰ centuries*. In the majority of such housesthere were shops on the ground floor and a flat for the family on the first floor. The urban development after 1872 neglected these buildings and as of today, only their messengers can be found nearby the House of Invalids *(181)*.

183

184

Some savours of the Inner Town: accentuated buildings are stressed by *domed corners*. The nearer one is of the *University Library*, the farther one is of *a bank (185)*.

The transformation of the town into capital, later on to metropolis is mostly due to the financially established decisions made by the Committee of the Metropolitan Communal Works. It was set up in 1870 and its first task was to regulate the metropolitan section of the Danube. This is how the embankments, avenues, boulevards streets, squares and the already mentioned public buildings were born. *Miklós Ybl planned the bank* and this spectacular *staircase* praises his work *(186)*.

However, some values have remained from previous ages, e.g. the *Franciscans' Church*. Their first church had already been built around 1250 at this place, the edge of the town at that time. Later on the temple became a mosque bearing the name of Sinan Bey and after the chase of the conquerors, the friars returned here and the actual temple was consecrated in 1743. The *high altar (188)* also originates from this period and is decorated with the statues of Franciscan saints and the two principal apostles, Peter and Paul. The altar was set up from the donation by Antal Grassalkovich, the aristocrat building the Gödöllő Palace.

Opposite to the temple a public draw-well was replaced with the composition of the *Nereids' Well* - completed in 1835 *(189)*.

185

186

In the surroundings of the temple several buildings stand from different ages. The richest one is the *former Savings Bank* on the opposite side. It was built at the beginning of the 1900s with a peculiar façade presenting oriental taste, with fancy towers and a special passage, the *'Paris Arcades' (190)*.

The Inner Town has been worked out, even as for the details. Some kind of *decoration* appears on the smaller surfaces *of the façades*, either figural, or only ornamental *(187)*.

187

189

188

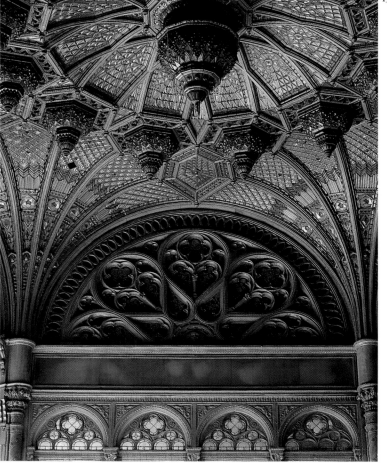

190

The *oldest part of Pest* can be discovered at the abutment of the Elisabeth Bridge, which was rebuilt in the mid-1960s *(195)*. It consists of *two consecutive squares* with names referring to their connection. The smaller one bears the name of *Sándor Petőfi*, the poet-major and victim of the 1848–49 revolution and war of independence *(193)*. The larger *Március 15. (15th March) Square* opens from here reminding of the date on which the revolution broke out.

A *counter-fortress* of the Roman defence system stretching southwards along the river from Aquincum was situated here to defend the crossing-point. Its remains are displayed in a smaller museum.

Beside that the *Parish-church of the Inner Town* stands with its simple Baroque façade, as its towers and the connecting parts were built in the first half of the 18th century *(192)*. The building itself is an alloy of several ages and styles: a most rustic part of the wall proves that a temple was standing here as early as at the beginning of the 11th century. The remains of St. Gellért, the Hungarian martyred bishop, are also kept here.

The development of the city in the 13th and 14th centuries and the growing riches of its

191

192

citizens contributed to the enlargement and reconstruction of the church.

The *sanctuary* took its shape at the end of the 14th century *(191)*. Its sedilia and the trecento wall-pictures clearly present the influence of the Italian art in the 14th century. The Italian Renaissance is also indicated by two ciboria made of red marble in 1507. Different ages left their marks on the church: the square of the congregation and the two statues originate from the 18th century, the pulpit reminds of the 19th century, and finally, the *winged altar (191)* recalling the spirit of the Middle Ages introduces the ecclesiastical art of the 20th century, as it has been painted by *Pál Molnár C.*, one of the artists from the so-called School of Rome.

194

193

195

The citizens of Pest due to the slow consolidation and development after the Turkish era enriched the town and the sight of the streets with churches and houses. While the churches have survived without exception, most of the *houses of the 18th century* standing on rather valuable sites disappeared. They were demolished at the time of the prosperity at the beginning and rather at the end of the 19th century. Some of them, however, remained thus the *Péterffy Palace* built in 1755 with beautiful gates and arms. Since 1831 a restaurant has been functioning in the building *(194)*.

Different faces of the Inner Town are shown in the pictures: the one of almost 200 years ago, the one of the Middle Ages, the one of the 18th century and when looking around abundant sights can be found from the last century, too.

In Budapest *Váci Street* has a special significance. Its names were earlier Great and Main Street, then 'Great mahalle' by the Turks, but its duty was always to link the northern and southern gates of the town, where the roads set out towards Belgrade and Bratislava along the Danube.

Most of its houses were built in the 19th and in the first decade of the 20th centuries *(196)*. Some of them lived more then one and a half hundred years, others were born during the big upswing, some of them imitate the palaces of Venice, others choose the cooler

196

197

198

Neoclassicism. Thus, the street is colourful and it is worthy to have a look upwards.

The street is *serving primarily its guests*: one can sit out and enjoy the colourful bustle or one can buy delicate things *(197)*, and behind a wonderful *Secessionist portal* marvels of flowers wait for the visitors in the atmosphere of one hundred years ago *(199, 200)*.

The shopping precinct continues *beyond the Elisabeth Bridge (198)*. This is as beautiful as the other, there is church and monas-tery with Baroque altars and pulpits, and as it is enywhere else in the Inner Town, the cavalcade of different styles is typical.

Váci Street is parallel with the Danube and the crossing streets generally starts at the river. It is worth walking along these,too, because they lead mostly to the famous *'Dunakorzó'*, the promenade, from where the best panorama opens on Buda, the Castle Hill, the bridges and the river. Significant public edifices can also be found here, e.g. an orthodox church, some reputable hotel, but the promenade was built basically for walking and enjoyment of the sight.

199

200

201

The square in the heart of the Inner Town takes its name from Mihály Vörösmarty, the leading personality of the lyric poetry in the 19th century. One and a half hundred years ago the square was called Deutsche Theather Platz, it bore hardly for a year the name of the president of the republic and, before and after that, the name of Francis Joseph's daughter, Gizella. It has to be noticed quickly, however, that with this choice the Emperor meant to commemorate the wife of the first King, St. Stephen. At the centre of *Vörösmarty Square* stands *the statue of its eponym since 1908 (202)*.

The pride of the square is *the Gerbeaud Confectionery and Café (203)*. Emil Gerbeaud, the Swiss confectioner and chocolate factory owner had worked in Hungary since 1884. Having invented the cognac-filled cherry bonbon he joined the confectionery of Henrik Kugler, operating here. The Café is famous for its atmosphere and pastries, but also for maintaining the one-hundred-years old spirit with its furniture, *interior design* and hospitality *(201)*. There were attempts to rename it 'Vörösmarty', but the citizens of Pest insisted on 'Zserbó' – this way, phonetically – because this was a notion. In wintertime or on cooler days, in the spring or autumn behind its windows, or in the summer on its terrace one can enjoy the bustling city and on the table the house-made pastries, ice-creams, parfaits and ... Who has not been in Váci Street or at Vörösmarty Square, has not been in Pest at all .

202

There might be years or decades in the life of every nation, when on searching for the identity and the historical roots they arrive at a national-type architecture. That is how was in Hungary and almost all over Europe in the 19th century, and still it is in some countries. This feature exists, nevertheless doesn't exist. It does exist, because the land, the conventions and the material are specific and all these three are substantial components of the architecture.

In the 1850s Frigyes Feszl and his followers thought the period from the foundation of the state until the very end of the 15th century was the rising and golden age of the Hungarians. If so, by drawing from this period the Hungarian-style architecture can be created. The *Vigadó*, this particular institution was built in this spirit to become the scene of balls, performances and restaurants *(206)*. It was considered as typically Hungarian, because it broke boldly with the Neoclassicism and reminded of the Middle Ages with its appearance, the *world of the Hungarian tales* with its frescoes *(205)*, the entertainment function with its relieves. It was an unusual building of its age, but the idea came back at the end of the 19th century and appeared on the works of Lechner.

The Vigadó was almost fully destroyed during the senseless siege of Budapest in the last weeks of 1944, a part of it had to be demolished, then it was restored successfully and

204

205

given back its original *cultural functions* – the balls, exhibitions, concerts – complying with the tradition, as Ferenc Liszt, Wagner, Brahms, Strauss, Bartók and Kodály also performed and conducted here *(204)*.

Budapest says goodbye in style with an aerial photograph of the *Inner Town* from the Castle District – an area selected by the UNESCO for increased protection. The picture is meaningful, it makes perceptible the role of the Danube, shows the hotels overlooking the Royal Palace and the Buda hills, it suggests the great urban development concept, that started with the ordering of the *embankments (207)*. It has already been learnt, that there is the Castle District below together with the Royal Palace, the medieval and the Baroque civic houses and the stone laced Matthias Church. It has been proven, that the history of the city dates back to two thousands years, as well as the heritage bequeathed to us by the ancient Roman, Turkish, German and Hungarian citizens is extremely colourful.

Almost two million inhabitants of the capital live in the houses and work, celebrate and keep on bustling in the city, but that is, what the photography finds difficult to cope with. It is similarly hard to reflect atmosphere, flavours, scents and experiences on the pages of a picture book. What else can be done: to come back and come again, either to Budapest or other regions of the country.

206

207